INSPIRED
POETRY
WRITINGS

REV. WILLIAM E. SMITH
ANNAPOLIS, MD

Order this book online at www.trafford.com
or email orders@trafford.com

Most Trafford titles are also available at major online book retailers.

Print information available on the last page.

ISBN: 978-1-4120-3550-7 (sc)
ISBN: 978-1-4907-9487-7 (hc)
ISBN: 978-1-4122-0553-5 (e)

Trafford rev. 04/30/2019

Trafford
PUBLISHING® www.trafford.com

North America & international
toll-free: 1 888 232 4444 (USA & Canada)
fax: 812 355 4082

But *there* is a spirit in man:
and the inspiration of the Almighty
giveth them understanding.

Job 32:8

Table Of Poetry

BOOK SEARCH

Keywords when searching on Internet: "Seek and ye shall find, knock and the door shall be open"

ABOUT THE BOOK

This book is a book of inspirational poems. To make you laugh, cry and to make you happy. This book is a book that can be read by all ages. It will surely make your day a day of excitement, laughter and of great pleasure.

TEASER

Do you love Poetry? Have you read this book? It's Inspirational, Hilarious, Realistic, and Exciting. You will love what's inside. Turn the pages. Try it you might like it.

Author's Biographical Note:

"About the Author"

Smith, William E.
[Pen] Willie, Smitty; [b.] December 12, 1952 Calvert County, MD,;[p.] Allen E. and Eva Q. Smith [m.] Gladys J. Contee, December 24, 1973; [ch.] Dion William; [ed.] Calvert Senior High, External Studies, Moody Bible Inst.; [occ.] I.F. I. Certified Drycleaner, United States Naval Academy Annapolis, MD; [memb.] Pastor, Restoration Temple Inc., Ordained Elder, Presiding Elder, Fourth Episcopal Diocese, Kings Apostle Church World Ministries, Inc. Annapolis, MD. Treasurer of the General Elders Board., Member of the Holiness Ministers Alliance, Inc. and Adjoining States; [hon.] Performance Award, U.S.N.A., Perfect Attendance Award State of MD. Faithful and Consecrated Service Award K.A.H.C. Certificates, Moody Bible Institute; In June 2005, Graduated from the North Carolina College of Theology earning an Associates Degree and a Graduate of Art in Biblical Studies and is currently pursuing Masters. Ordained Deacon Credential, Ordained Ministers License, and Elder Credential. [oth.writ.] Song lyrics, music, copyrighted Library of Congress, Poetry copyrighted, Library of Congress, Washington D.C. made International Poet through Noble House Publishers.; London, New York, Paris. 2003 and 2004.; Poem entitled the Eagle Flies, won International recognition in Europe as well. Was published in [2] books.; Theatre Of The Mind, and Colours Of The Heart, a distinguished Member of the International Society of Poets. Has been Published also in National Anthologies of Poetry and has been presented the Editor's Choice Award for Outstanding Achievement in Poetry through the International Library of Poetry 2004.

Acknowledgements

I wish to express my deepest thanks to the following persons:

Mrs. Gladys Contee-Smith, my wife, who was there when I needed her assistance in typing and proofreading. Dion W., my son, for sacrificing his time.

Ms. Vanessa Contee-Brown, who never failed me when the manuscript needed to be typed from the very beginning. Her expertise was indispensable in bringing this initial work to print.

Ms. Agnes Hunter, who also is a writer in her own right, for her advice as well as encouragement.

Brother Robert Green Jr., my best friend who's always there for me.

Mr. Donald Smith, co-worker who encouraged me from the beginning to the very end. He could barely wait for the book to be published.

Ms. Oreal Morsell, my cousin, who was helpful with the final proofreading.

Sister Tia McCoy, thank you so much for all your assistance.

Finally, Bishop and Mrs. James Colter Sr. for their encouraging words. Bishop Wilbert L. Baltimore, my Senior Bishop and Presiding Prelate, Kings Apostle Church World Ministries, Inc., and Bishop Bette E. Funn of the Fourth Episcopal Diocesan for their Prophetic word.

May God Bless you all!

Dedicated to

My Mother

Mrs. Eva Q. Smith, whose love, faith, and devotion to God encourages my heart through the life she now lives before me.

And to My (Deceased) Father

Mr. Allen E. Smith, for having faith and confidence in me while in ministry to the very end. He will always be remembered.

Foreword

After many years of hard work, studying, and waiting for the opportunity to make a decision, William finally concluded that; planning and setting goals pay off. He made up his mind to pursue such a task of fulfilling a dream that one day would come true. Through much prayer and confidence within himself, he took the long journey to accomplish a dream. With much sacrifice and dedication, he would not deter from the faith. So he brings to this work something different, something inspired, hilarious and exciting. Only because of his inspired vision, a new life of poetry has been birthed in a new generation of people across America and throughout the United Kingdom, for this cause. Poetry has become realistic in the hearts and minds of the rich and the poor, Blacks and Whites. It has become the true meaning of life in realistic terms. It also reaches the hearts of all races, young and old. Therefore, William's love for people, commitment and dedication sends a strong message to all of us, that poetry is alive! And that it will never die. It will not cease the moment to fulfill someone's dreams.

Bro. Robert J. Green, Jr.

Introduction

To God be the glory-many years passed waiting for this opportunity. However, when God saw that the season was right, He gave me words of inspiration and laughter during my years of listening to the many voices of everyday situations. I thought it would be interesting for me to write about experiences and what I had heard with the listening ear. By watching and observing those things that I saw placed a very persistent goal in my mind.

I've been encouraged for many years to publish my manuscript. Yet, I've not done so, because the time and the season had not come. It was back in 1968 that I felt a call to write. I started writing Song Lyrics and Poems of various types, which led to Poetry. There were many times I felt like giving up, but there was an inspirational drive in me to continue the long journey and to fulfill a dream that someday may come true. Though I had many ups and downs, I heard the voice of a Holy God saying to me, "You can do all things. Keep the Faith."

What you are about to read now is inspired writings that only come through inspiration. I could not have written these poems without the quiet, still voice of Almighty God whispering in my ear. I believe gifts are from God. I also believe that as you read, you will be able to identify with or relate to something that you have seen, heard, or experienced.

I hope that you'll find a sense of humor in reading some of these collected poems. In doing so, I pray that as you give some thought to them, you will soon discover your talent or God-given gift and allow the Holy Spirit to reveal to you how to publicize or share your gift.

May God Bless You

I Ain't Goin' Back

I ain't goin' back
I've come too far now!
Just ain't worth a dime goin' back
It would be hard to trace over my tracks

There were some rough places
And I've forgotten many faces
There would be some tears
That would never dry up for years
Some frowns that would never leave.

I've climbed to the top of the hill
There I see hope ahead instead
A sun shiny day awaits me
As the heavens bare before me
I ain't goin' back

Time doesn't allow me
To turn back for nothin'
I've gained my freedom from fear
I ain't goin' back

My foot has become swift
Like a horse running a battle
My eyes are bright, and crystal clear
I can see tomorrow
I ain't goin' back.

Mama's Gone   Part I

Father to his son,
Son, Mama's gone
And you and I are left alone
Life has been wonderful
No longer have to sleep on the floor
Company can come to the front door
Don't have to be embarrassed anymore
I've peace and sweet rest
Now that I've the best
I no longer have to confess

Ain't there joy in this home?
Color TV, VCR in every room
Good old music, blasting from my stereo
Coca-Cola running through my veins
No worries to wreck my brain

Son, Mama's gone
And she ain't a comin' back
Now don't you leave me alone?
I need you to stay home
Empty the trash, cut the wood
And answer the phone
Pay the bills, and bring me my meals
Drive me around
I've gotta enjoy myself now before I die
Because there ain't no pie in the sky.

(Continue to Son to Father)

Son to Father   Part II

Dad Just because Mama's gone
You don't have to treat me wrong
I don't want to leave you alone
But you're working my fingers to the bone
I get tired of answering the phone
And keep listening to your same old tune.

I cannot take it any more
You may be having yourself a ball
But that's not all
Let me tell you something before I go
I just get tired of sleeping on the floor
I'm gone, gone, gone
Won't forget to lock the door.

Empty Life

My whole life seems to be sinking
Dripped ink from a pen
Used, splattered over and over again
Wasted with hopeless fears and years
Thrown in the trash on paper
Waiting to be burned.

Refined with pleasures and colors
No one will ever know
Empty pitchers drained water from the faucet
Pretending not to be noticed
Like-ba-bush-ka grandmother dim
A unicorn, a mythical animal

Va-moose transient, never to return
Flung to and fro, no dwelling place
Empty life, an untrue story
Only a trace remains
A pathway through a dark tunnel, leads to nowhere
Darkness is brought to surface
And light no longer remains
An empty life of pain, and nothing to gain.

I'm Just a Soldier

I'm just a Soldier
In the army of the Lord
I've heard the voice of God's command
Your works are not in vain
Everything that you do for me
There's nothing to lose
But much to gain

I'm on the battlefield
With my sword and my shield
And when my life is over
God will say, "peace be still"
I must work the works
Of Him that sent me
Until my days are done
For my determination is to see
The Father and the Son

I give all my life to Jesus
My time is in His hands
To every girl and boy
To every woman and man
For God has called me to work
And so, then, I must do
By showing my love to others
Because His words are true.

Paper Stamp

Travel taste good sweet glue
Licked placed on paper, white
Flat and smoothed out
Hands of every color
Smashed, wrinkled and worn
Stamped and sealed
Leave no trace
Maybe someone will receive
How far not always remembered
Long the days dark the nights thunder
Turning corners, and curves, lines, streets
Carried and tossed to the side-roads
Waiting for its final resting place there
Awakening to a new day sunset rises
Residence, someone known smiles.

An Inspiration of Trust

You're an inspiration of trust
Like the Banks of Sweden
Where my money will never rust
And interest remains always
I can always make deposits
And receive a return
For you're an inspiration of trust

You're an inspiration of trust
Like a safe security box
An ATM machine, still
Always waiting to receive my number
Only if I can remember
When I give my all to you,
You're always there to see me through
For you're an inspiration of trust.

Faith Stands the Storm

I've been knocked down, pushed around
Walked over and trodden
I've been bruised, but not forgotten
My soul is anchored in Jesus alone
My faith stands the storm
Although the devil tries to do me harm

I've been upside, downside
My face pointed towards the sky
For my Lord to come, to carry me home
As my days busted towards dawn rise
Hears melodies of songs of heaven sing
Let freedom ring let freedom ring
Down in my bosom I cry
My eyes watered with tears of pain
Nothing to lose, but much to gain
My faith stands the storm.

Getting Old

I'm getting old
As the days go by
You ask me why my hair is white
I can tell you the reason why.

When I look back over my life
At all the years that's gone by
I can tell you one thing
I'm not alone.

I'm not what I use to be
And I'm not trying to be, you see
Keep on having birthdays
And you will be just like me.

William Smith

Sing a Song of America

Sing a song of America
Whose interest rates have risen
Whose stock market has fallen?
Sing a song of America
No positive answers or decisions

Peace no longer lives among us
Our world leaders no longer can we trust?
Sing a song of America
Whose beauty no more we see
Enslaved by injustice
And we no longer are free

Sing a song of America
Whose love has faded?
And drugs have invaded
Whose prayers are no longer in schools?
Forgotten the golden rules

Sing a song of America
Whose prejudice will never end?
A world full of hatred and fear
Ah' we need peace, my friend.

Just a Touch

Just a touch of your hand
Electrifies my soul
Lights up my eyes
And sets my soul on fire
I know that you're sincere
Because you always
Enhance my very desire

Just a touch of your hand
Moves me to think
Motivates me to concentrate
To find words that penetrate
All because of a touch
Never, ever evaporate

Now that I can still feel
That your touch is real
I can always take time
To hold your hand
And never walk away again.

Liberty of a Nation

Liberty of a Nation
Need not an invasion
But an embracing, and persuasion
People are dying
Why others are crying
I want to be free

Liberty of a Nation
Violence and crimes
Bankruptcy and insolvency
Fraudulent lending practices and indecency
A Nation that's in need of an emergency
Capitalism, nationalism, no patriotism
Destruction of national sovereignty

Liberty of a Nation
Embodiment of evil within itself
A voice crying in the wilderness
Cocaine, narcotics, and riots
Daughters against mothers
Fathers against sons
We have nowhere to turn.

My Will

Had I not known you long ago
I would've swept you
From off of your feet
And never left you broken hearted
Lying in the open street
My will, I would've included you
But, to tell you the honest truth
I left it to my cat named Sue.

Between the Lines

Hoping to see you
Between the lines of life and death
Had we but words and years test
And never, ever raised a voice
While time, nights of restless hours
Between the pillow of tears rest

Your blue eyes look toward me
Speaking soft words of love unfazed
Trying to find every wit
To say I love you still

Nights after nights I lay beside you
Your hair so black like coffee
While your kisses gentle sweet
I can remember touching your hands
And words of love repeat

Hoping to see you
Between the lines of life and death
Had upon my bed of peaceful rest
And never, ever shed a tear
While time, days has come and gone
When life on earth has disappeared.

William Smith

A Broken Empty Glass

Let me die the death,
Of the righteous
And leave me behind nothing to fight
But my name and what is right
Only my voice once to remember
And a seat of comfort
And splendor thunder
Beneath the shadow of my past
Only a broken empty glass.

Memories That Last

Days that pass
I often think about
The memories that last
When I met you years ago
My love is still the same
May be older, gray and wrinkle
But I can bear the pain

Memories that last
I often think about yesterday
Now, that it is gone
And you I still own

As each day goes by
I ask myself, the reason why?
I'm still in love with you
No matter what you do
Memories that never fade away
Maybe that's the reason why I stay

Never ever find another like you
Whose love for me, has always been true
Like emerald glue
Always holding each other together
Memories that will never let go, ever.

Who Am I

Born in a world unknown
Lost of understanding
Delivered by the doctor's hands
Laid by my mother's side
Who am I?

A stranger, an infant baby,
Born, I cry.
I cry for peace
I struggle for life
And unwanted certainties
I cannot see yesterdays past,
Or tomorrow's future
Who am I?

I do not know
I find myself,
In the center of a new beginning
I see images and reflections
Moving objects and possibilities
Who am I?

Born in a world unknown
But yet, not alone
I see lights of all colors
And faces, shades, and smiles

Who am I?
I'm an infant, with no sense of direction
No remembrance of thought
No understanding of life
Only the feeling to be loved
Born in a world unknown.

Secret Love

I've never, ever told you
You were mine
Although I've embraced you
And you belonged to another

Your face shines like silk
Your eyes glitter like the morning light
You were young, amusing, and tarnished
With color, bright.

Your hair's dusty and black, like coffee
Your voice mutters deep, like the river Spain.
You let me take, and hold your hands
I caressed you in my arms
While we were on the Caribbean Island, West Indies.

No one knew our secret love
One thousand times, I'd kissed you
Although momentarily, misunderstood
You kept aiming at my heart
I gazed but little I thought
The waves of the sea danced
And the waters leaped
And clapped their hands with praise.

The moon was shining,
And smiling in the night sky
As I smelled fresh perfume
Upon your breast, there we lie

Upon the old ship
That left San Antonio, Texas
Just you and I alone
So! No one will ever know
Where our secret love has gone.

Yesterday's Past

I've never thought I'd live this long
Like an old legacy or song
Wrote on a piece of paper
Traced by a publisher whose now dead.

I've out grown my wrinkles and frowns
No more worries upon my face
I've nothing to dread
But that I've found cannot be replaced.

So I smile to keep looking happy
Watching the lines in the mirror
Upon my face, grow.

An image of yesterday's picture
Hangs on the wall behind me
Only what I use to be, I see.

Painted by the Master's hands
A creation of yesterday's past
A face of moi-re and gloss
Glowing, glittering, and classic
I see through the mirror clearly
A mortal of yesterday's past.

Let Me Die

Let me die the death of the righteous
Let me be counted among the stars
Where no trouble is
Where the moon shines so bright
And the sun gives off a radiant light
Above the place of restless night.

Let me die the death of the righteous
Let my soul rest in peace
Away from pain and sorrow grief
Let my eyes see God's beauty
And my spirit goes free to thee
Let my heart of sweet relief
Away from days that tested my faith
I no longer have to wait
When the time comes, I must move on
To my grave from dust to dawn.

Woman to Husband

I'm tired of living with you
You're black, but you act so blue
Your voice like the sea that roars
Eyes full of lightning
Your heart full of venom
Flooding your veins
Act like a drunken man
But not insane
You moo like a cow in the stall
A wild horse galloping on a dusty trail
Unbalance, unstable, good for nothing
And I'm praying oh' God
Hurry up, and just do something.

What A Surprise

I thought I'd married a princess
Whose royal seat I would have shared
With beautiful golden slippers
And long pretty hair
But once I brought her home
And she took off her clothes
What I thought I had
Nobody even knows.

Don't Cry

When you see me, passing by
With another cutie in my car
Don't cry, or even ask why?
There's no alibi
I've found someone that treats me like gold
Young and pretty;
And not too old.

O' God, Mighty in Strength

O' God, mighty in strength
Thou presence is everywhere
Whom by the hands the heavens were made
Everything in its proper place
The universe, you did create
And all that's within
For in the beginning of thou creation
There were but no sin.

O' God, mighty in strength
How easy it is to forget
Sometimes we take life for granted
And never stop to think
Who commanded the sun to shine?
To show us the way
O' God mighty in strength
Guides us through the day

O' God mighty in strength
Thou takes man by the hand
Leads him through dangerous tolls
And carries him through this land
Upholding all things
By thy mighty strength
If man would only stop to think
How mighty a God we serve
Would soon come to repentance
And let his voice be heard.

The Mistress

How gallant is the mistress
Who sought to entrap thee!
With her glamour gleam of wit
Her sweet perfume of intelligence
Never annoyed her inclination to quit
As she ambles, and warps her hips.

How irksome is the Mistress
Who aims to trample thy repute!
With her splendor perfection of beauty
Her captivating smiles of certainty
Never ponder about her boldness to refute
As she endures, to wink her eyes.

How reluctant is the Mistress
Who sought to engulf passing strangers!
With her enticing words of shrewd intrigue
Her persistency, ungodly appetite
Never resistible, always throbbing
As she poses, on the streets potency
To capture her prey in the night.

Old Joe Wimp

Old Joe Wimp
Wasn't no pimp
Wherever he went, he always limped
His hair was long, stinky and gray
Smelled like fish scales on a sun shiny day

Smoked a pipe
From the side of the mouth
The benches in the park
Were his bed and his house

One leg long, one leg short
He would leave you behind
Just give him a start

He leaned, he walked
With handmade poles
He wore old shoes that had no soles

His beard was long
Hung down to his toes
He wore freckles
On the left side of his nose

His eyes were blue
His pupils were red
Everyone knew him,

William Smith

Thought he was dead
But old Joe Wimp
Had nothing to dread

M C Hammer psyched him up a bit
But old Joe Wimp
Was too legit to quit!

William Smith

Woman to Her Second Husband

You may stand tall
As big as you can
But if you hit me
You'll be less than a man

You may cuss, fuss
And raise the sane
But if you hit me
Look out fryin' pan

You may jerk, flirt
And mess around
But if you hit me
I'm gonna knock you down

If you think I'm afraid of you
Open your eyes the jokes on you

If you hit me, you better run
Look out gun
Bang, bang, bang here I come

If you think I'm gonna run from you
Look out grave
Cause I'm burying you too!

William Smith
Smoker, Stop Smokin'

Smoker, stop smokin'
Cause it ain't no joke
Keep on puffing
You're bound to get choked

Smoker, stop smokin'
Cause you'll shorten your life,
With all that pain, misery and strife
One more draw on that cigarette
May lead you to bad health
If you don't quit

Smoker, stop smokin'
Cause you're taking a chance
Cancer isn't no picnic or no romance
If you don't want to live very long
Keep smokin' those cigarettes
And you'll be long gone

Smoker, stop smokin'
Stop kidding yourself
Cause you ain't fooling, no one else
I've told you once, I'll tell you twice
Keep on smokin', you gonna lose your life!

Love Sick

You may write me a letter
And call it a day
You may tell me you don't love me
But that will not keep me away

Have you found someone else
That causes you to blossom and bloom?
Or some crazy idiot
To light up your room?
But that will not keep me away

You may curse me out, round and about
Or sift me like wheat won't make me shout
Or yell, scream, lose your voice
But that will not keep me away

I'm here to stay come whatever may
Hang up the phone, I will still pay
I'll call you even if you don't talk
I'll catch a cab or even walk
Whatever it takes to make this last
I'll do my best to hold fast.

I'll hold on to the phone
I'll walk alone,
I'll spend my last dime
I'll take out the time
I'll wait for you, to make up your mind
If it takes forever
I'll still be on the line.

William Smith

I Know What Makes You Tick

From the early morning rise
To the evening tide
I know what makes you tick
Columbia coffee, caffeine free
Black and thick
For that's the only thing
That really, really
Will make you tick.

Dark Ages of the Past

Dark ages of the past
Time has gone at last
Years have come, my soft hair
Gray an' old as clay
Brightnin' the future for tomorrow
With its wisdom of today

Where are you, with your blue sky?
Dark ages of the past!
Time just flies by
Oh! How rough the road, I've toiled
Ah, the heavy load I've borne
My feet have trodden

Ain't gotta put up with you
My smooth skin has broken
My eyes no longer see yesterday
Footsteps slower than before
Can't turn back no more

Dark ages of the past
Time waits not for me
I'm a man, wanna be free
But I cry, my feet a' achin'
I'm worried and tired

I stood upon the graves of great warriors
Great heroes of faith
Scented the negative ness of freedom

Tasted sadness and pain
Looked toward the future
Crossed the dusty plain

Dark ages of the past
My fingers I've worked to the bone
Ain't gonna leave you alone

(Continued next page)
Where were you?
I've shed some tears
Through the years
Sat in the back seats of buses
In the darkness of the hour
Still had no power

A new day a-comin'
I see afar off
To the distance trail
And I see the beauty of a new city
I'm tired!
But I ain't givin' up
Nope, I won't look back
There's nothin' behind me
Can't you see! I'm free
Hope has been born anew
Falls down upon my head
Like dew

Dark ages of the past
Can't you see! I'm free
You held my hand tight
Wouldn't let it go
I fought for myself
But you wouldn't open the door
I've climbed rough and rugged hills,
looked back at the past
Time for me, Uh! Just wouldn't last

Drinker my water from the wells
Watched the wheel of saw mills
As they spin
Cut wood with an axe
Which I thought was a sin
Look here!
Look at me
It hasn't been easy
But thank God, I'm free!
Do you remember me?

When I Die

When I die
Just lay me in the grave
And let me stay
Don't just cry your life away
When my cold body has decayed
I will awaken
On that great judgment day!

Your Love

When I look at you
I see something so wonderful
When you smile
I see something so sweet
When I touch your hands
I feel something so warm
Not your eyes that keep me hanging on
But something so charming,
Your love

I search for something
Within the mind
When I do, I hear each beat of your heart
But a little more than that
I feel the kindness of real truth
And the world beyond
Your love

William Smith

Love Is Like a Shining Star

Love is like a shining star
It shines afar in you
In the darkest hour of the night
It glows so bright

Like taking a shower
Always blossoms like a flower
Sends a scent of sweet odor
That no one can resist
Takes its toll from the start
And pierces the very heart

Love is like a shining star
No matter where you are
It reaches out with a smile
Hangs in the sky
Goes on for miles and miles
That never end around the bend
Reaches out to embrace
Like bright lights
That shine upon one's face
Always has a beginning
But never has an end.

William Smith

Dearest Love

My dearest love
No other love, could ever give me
The happiness and bliss
My dearest love
That I can get from you
And your enduring kiss
To me is like a bush of red roses
My dearest love

To show how much I care
So by my actions
I'll make you more aware
Forever, and forever I will love you
Yes! Because to me,
You're just like an angel

The years we have been together
Ah! So faithful and true
So full of love and much cheer
It makes me feel always happy
When you are near

No other love, when the final curtain falls
Together we will be
Sharing endless moments of pleasure
Throughout eternity

56

William Smith

You're graceful and kind
Beautiful and fine and
You're mine
Together we will stand
Hand in hand
Until we reach our destiny
There forever we will always be.

Nowhere to Run, Nowhere to Hide

You can run, but you can't hide
There is nothin' you can do
God knows all about you
And your bad habits, too.
Hears every word you say
Watches you and I every day.
You may run and hide,
Behind the old oak tree
But God will surely see.

You go to the supermarket
Get in with the crowd
But someone else will see you
And say!
Why are you very loud?
Who are you running from
To make you act like that?
Is it a snake or a rat?
Or Miss Sally's big fat cat?

You can run, but you can't hide
God knows where you are.
There is no need to run
You won't get very far
You better get your house in order
Your soul saved from sin
God is surely a comin'
He's just around the bend.

Call on Jesus

Sometimes I get so worried
Until I don't know what to do
I just call on Jesus
He always sees me through.
I lift up my head to heaven
And say a little prayer
He whispers in my ears
And tells me He's always there.

So! Every time I have a problem
I always stop to pray
I just call on the name of Jesus
He always makes a way.

I Thank You Lord

Every night before I go to bed
I thank you Lord, for my daily bread
I thank you Lord for watching over me
Opening my eyes so that I can see
Giving me hands so that I can pray
For taking care of me both night and day.

William Smith

Why Don't You Go to Bed

Why do you sit up all night?
And scratch your nappy head
When you already know
You must go to bed

You just a wasting your time
Be tired when mornin' come
And might get left behind
Better to be late than never
Cause I ain't changing my mind

The train will be a' rolling
Fast and down the track
If you miss that train
Don't you come back!

The taxi will be a' rolling
But you must pay your fare
And if you miss that taxi
The bus will carry you there

To work you must go
Sleepy, tired or not
If the boss man sees you sleeping
He'll fire you on the spot.

Gift of Love

Oh! Lord I thank thee
For the gift of love,
That you have given to me
To share this gift to everyone
So the world can truly see.

William Smith

Bedtime

Dark the night, the day is spent
It's time to go to bed
I love you Mama for all you do
That's all that I can say
You washed my face, and combed my hair
Your love you gave to me
Taught me how to say my prayer
Now, I lay me down to sleep.

A Mama's Love

Dear Mama,
I love you
For all you say and do.
You told me that you loved me
And every word is true.
When I call for you to help me,
You come to see about me.
A Mama's love is pure!
You are always by my side
No matter what I need you for
You never run and hide.

I Praise You Lord

Dear Lord,
I kneel in prayer
To talk to you.
I know there is no secret
What you can do.
You protect me, each and everyday
You guide my footsteps all the way
So! I praise you Lord, with all my heart
Because of your wonderful thought.

Not Shall We Stand Tall

The earth is filled with crystals tall
When it rains-not yet it falls
Thunder roars, the lightening sparks
In front of the wind, voices bark
Down the road I walked, standing tall
Separating the leaves of autumn fall
But yet --

The earth is filled with crystals tall
But not shall we stand tall
The world is filled with blazing fire
Extract emotions, pleasures of desire
Heaven is a home of peace
In the sky, it hangs like a Christmas wreath
Sin not I be for God made love for me.

And at the corner of the street
The showers beat, not yet it rain
War starts, we fight in vain
But yet --
We are a people of a great world
The world of the Almighty God
A world filled with crystals tall
Not shall we stand tall.

The Nightmare

I, visionary, envisioned a creation of the imagination
It was a dream
Dreadfulness and frightfulness grew upon me
Breathing laboriously to catch my breath
Strange, fearless as I panic in my being
Every heartbeat heard
Blinded as my eyes kept silently closed
Strange feeling of depression and stress

I experienced a sensation of the mind
So emotional, I couldn't keep still
Too true to be real
Too real to be true
I awaken from a very long sleep
It was not a dream, but a nightmare.

Mortgage Due

Phone rang half past two
Bill collector said,
"Your mortgage is due;
You're four mortgages behind,
And we haven't received a dime.
I said, "I don't have any money."
He laughed! And thought it was funny
Told me if you don't have it by seven,
You are going to be put out by eleven.

A Brighter Day

If you stay in the presence of God
And do what His words say
You'll find a brighter tomorrow
You'll see a better day

Stop and listen to the Spirit
What the Spirit always says
He'll never leave you astray
Follow that narrow pathway
You'll surely get home someday

Jesus will meet you there
In that city
So bright and fair
You'll find a brighter tomorrow
You'll see a brighter day

Your home it will be forever
No sickness or sorrow never
You'll be happy as can be
With your Lord and Savior
You'll see
You'll have a brighter tomorrow
You'll see a better day.

Living To Live Again

I'm living to live again
In this old world full of sin
I gave my heart to Jesus
And he came right on in
I'm living to live again

For me to live is Christ
And to die is gain
I'm living to live again

It's appointed unto man
Once to die, let me tell you why
After death, the judgment surely will come
And I will see the Father and the Son

That's why I'm living to live again
Oh, yes! I'm living to live again
I'm living to live again.

My troubles will be over
My problems will come to an end
And my new life will just begin
I'll be living in heaven
With Jesus, my closest friend

In that mansion
In the sky
In that sweet by and by
I will reign with Him on high.

Teach Me How to Pray

Dear Lord, I'm worried
And don't know what to do
I'm asking, give me the strength
So that I can go through

My burdens seems so hard to bear
And I can't find an answer anywhere
Dear Lord, I'm calling
I'm calling on you.

I come to thee
Savior, the anchor of my soul
While the fountain of life overflows
Please! From day to day
Take my troubles away
And please! Teach me how to pray

Satan is on my track
Trying to turn me back
He's going to and fro
Seeking whom he may devour
And I need thee every hour
So let me feel thy Holy Ghost power

Teach me how to pray
Dear Lord, please! Teach me how to pray
I need you every step of the way
So teach me, teach me how to pray.

William Smith

He's Calling You

He's calling you, He's calling you
Jesus Christ is calling you.
Are you willing to pay the price
To receive eternal life?
Are you willing to go through?

He's calling you, He's calling you
Jesus Christ is calling you
He's calling you today
To teach sinners the way
He's calling you right now

He's calling you, He's calling you
Jesus Christ is calling you
Don't you wait too late to make up your mind!
If you don't listen, you'll be left behind

He's calling you, He's calling you
Jesus Christ, He's calling you
He'll speak softly to you
He'll tell you what to do
Jesus is calling you

Isaiah, the eagle eye prophet, had a vision
And he heard a voice speaking to him
Saying whom shall I send, and who will go for us
To heal the sick and to set the captive free?
Then Isaiah said, here am I
Send me, I'll go
I'll go to tell this people today

William Smith

He's calling you, He's calling you
Jesus Christ, He's calling you
Why don't you indeed, take heed today?
And listen to what God has to say.

Please Pardon Me

Oh' Lord I'm guilty
For all I've done wrong
I'm weak, but thou art strong

My iniquity is great before me
But oh' Lord
Open my eyes so that I can see

Oh' Lord won't you, please!
Pardon me
I'm blind and cannot see

Oh' Lord, hear my cry
And attend unto my prayer
I'm lonely and in despair

My life is passing away
Each and everyday
And Lord help me to say

Oh' Lord, please pardon me
I'm blind and cannot see
Won't you please pardon me?

Pardon me, dear Lord
Pardon me, I'm blind
And cannot see
Please! Won't you pardon me?

William Smith

I was young, but now!
I'm old
I'm seeking refuge for my soul
Please Lord, come to me
And please, pardon me!

Pretty Boy

Pretty boy ain't pretty no more
His girl friend threw him out
And locked the door
Cause pretty boy ain't pretty no more

Stayed out late
Five nights straight
His girl friend, locked the door -
And closed the gate
Cause pretty boy ain't pretty no more

He sat in the bars
And ran the streets
All he did-was cheat, cheat, cheat
Pretty boy ain't pretty no more

Broke in the house
Forgot to close the door
Girl friend hit him
With a wedge, and a hoe
Pretty boy just ain't pretty no more

Called the rescue squad
They came on the scene
Flashing their lights
Blowing their sirens
Gave him oxygen – that didn't work
All he did was jerk, jerk, jerk
Pretty boy ain't pretty no more

William Smith

They put him on a bed
Closed the door
Drove him to the hospital
Didn't come back no more
Pretty boy ain't pretty no more
He's dead, dead, dead.

I Do Not Know

My eyes look towards the blue sky
As my mind wonders beyond – beyond its galaxy

'Twas I was told at the end,
A pot of gold.
Maybe heaven, my friend.

No one knows, but how far
Maybe surpasses the eastern star
Or somewhere over the rainbow
Behind the clouds of planets,
The moon, the sun, the stars;
Maybe even Mars.

Where life ends, I do not know
When yesterday passes on,
And a new tomorrow begins.

Maybe a throne of pearls I'll see,
Heavenly angels, awaiting me.
With twenty-four elders;
Kneeling at the feet of God.
While the Saints all assembled,
On one accord.

Maybe songs of praises
Will they all sing.
Let freedom ring –
Let freedom ring.

(Continued next page)

William Smith

Let the angels rejoice.
And God be glorified.
Let the Elders shout victory,
And the Saints kneel unto thee.
For I've crossed over
In a land of promise.
Where no dark clouds will ever arise
For I've passed over to the other side.

I've reached my goal.
As I was told.
I've declared for my worried soul
Rest, sweet old rest
Triumphantly – I've passed the test.

Don't Panic

When your wife tells you
She doesn't love you anymore;
And when you find out
She ain't nothing but a whore
Don't panic.

When the lights go out
In the night;
When she accuses you
Of something that just ain't right
Don't panic.

When your bed becomes no more
A resting place;
And whatever you tell her
Becomes a disgrace;
And every word, cannot be replaced
Don't panic.

When you have tried everything
But cannot trace;
And your romantic years become a waste
Please, please, just don't panic.

William Smith

Tomorrow

I live in the past – but should I
Have thou a home in the present sky
As I look toward thee for common sense
To know that thou art in present tense

Each day brings together new meaning
New hopes become dreams and realities
I await to face tomorrow's promises
Knowing that life will be beaming

The years that have gone from thee
Nor close thy eyes to anxiously see
In my presence I shall rejoice
My soul in God set free

Tho' hills are rough and high to climb
When thou no longer can reach the top
I live today as no tomorrow
Maybe sing a song – a verse or two
Then awaken from sleepless dreams
While awaiting sunny days
And running streams.

The Murderer

A murderer in the streets to find
Once carried a loaded gun.
The moon gleams so bright to seek
While still, nowhere to run.

A policeman searches behind the scene,
Blowing a whistle loud.
A shepherd dog barks attentively,
Within the noisy crowd.

A helicopter probes through the woods.
Lights flash through the streams
Behind the trees of mid-night.
Disappearing out of sight.

Then the morning dawn arises.
The sun glitters bright.
There they discover the murderer,
Sleeping in broad daylight.

Street Lights

The streetlights shines
Where the sun doesn't shine
The playboy plays ball –
And sings nursery rhymes
The playboy ain't no friend of mine.

The cowgirl rides horses,
Plays hopscotch,
Daddy spends money –
That he just ain't got.

Mama stays home
Washes pots and pans –
Awaits for daddy to come home;
So she can raise sane.

The streetlights shines
Where the sun doesn't shine
Streetlights shine
Where the sun doesn't shine.

I Awoke, Up In Heaven

I awoke, up in Heaven
Thought I was in hell –
Resided such a profligate life
I was to witless to tell

God had mercy – mercy on me
His grace and mercy – set me free
I was so blind –
I just couldn't see

Because I awoke, up in Heaven
Thought I was in hell –
And the Lord had mercy
I was saved by the bell.

I'm so exulting
It betides to me
I was spiritually blind –
I merely could see
Hell would've been –
The place for me.
God had mercy – mercy on me.

Heaven

Heaven is a place
Where everyone would want to be
To die – and go to hell
Would be total misery

'Twas said – dying is easy
To go to hell – would be a sin
I rather accept Jesus as Lord
So I can make it in

Everyone wants to go to Heaven
But no one wants to die
Heaven is a prepared place
Somewhere beyond the sky

To die – and lose your soul
Would be a total shame
To avoid from going to hell
You must be born again.

Joe Blow

Joe Blow – didn't even know
That he was born
Crippled and poor
Joe Blow was his name.
That's the only way
He got his fortune and fame.

William Smith

The Kite

It flew so high in the air
Above my head - I could barely see
Beyond the sky into the clouds
A lost of memory.

Yet I stood there
On the ground
Blaming myself to see that little kite
Blown away
Left hopeless dreams for me.

Lost Dime

I never lost – but one dime
And it wasn't cognizant at all
Twice I found it unrepentantly
Sully in the soil.

Repeatedly, repeatedly – I misplace it
Though it was a friend of mine
If I had – but one dime.
I would lose it all the time.

The Divorcee

Sadness and sorrow
And days are now gone
My princess, my dearest
I'm left all alone.

Madness and dreadness
As the years go by
My life is now empty
And I often wonder why?

Tears and teardrops
Upon my pillow I cry
Hoping one day I soon will die.

To be with my lover
My friend, my wife
In Heaven with you
For the rest of my life.

No pain, no misery,
No solitude, no strife,
No hate, no fear
Forever my wife.

My Lady

My Lady is like perfume
Sweet as sugar - pure
Honey in a rock

Gentle as the summer breeze
Blowing swiftly across my bed of silk
On a cool evening in the spring

My Lady is like roses
Blossom colors, glittery leaves
Flashy fragments, artistic beauty

My Lady is like soft words
From an English poem
Written by a Poet's hand,
Young, steady, soft and smooth

Oh, she's like the Golden Gate Bridge
Hanging over the Pacific Ocean
Carrying me to my destiny

She's like the blood running
Through my veins – or else I die
My Lady is vigorous,
Brilliant, vehement
Never, ever changing – valiant

 (Continue next page)

Always there – unconditional
Concerned, intractable, and determined
Encouraging me to go on
She's black, beautiful, and strong
She's the melody to my song.

She's my road map
To which I travel
She's the direction to my path
Leading me to dreams of hope
No misery, no strife.

My Lady, my friend, my wife
She is my whole life – My Lady.

Cryin' Doesn't Pay

Cryin' all the time
Just doesn't pay
Can't get rid of those headaches
Just gotta pray

Cryin' all the time
Until your eyes turn red
Makes someone think you're almost dead

Cryin' all day – just doesn't pay
Just doesn't stop trouble
From coming your way
Stop cryin' – stop cryin'
Cryin' just doesn't pay!

William Smith

Laziness

All that laziness
Won't get you nowhere
All because you just don't care
You want someone to take care of you
I got news – It just won't do.

The Eagle Flies

Beneath the blue quiet storm
Sprinkling raindrops fall
Upon the golden days of summer
The voice of thunder calls

In the silent dew showers
The beauty of spring flowers
The eagle flies, cloudy skies

The eagle flies with sweeping wings
Her beak seeks the seawaters deep
Shattered the waves ocean air
Scattering its wings, feathers blow
Landing on its sandy shore

Blowing in the wind of natures face
God's unfailing autumn grace
Raindrops silence, sound
Wetting the gray rooftop shingles
Falling upon earth solid ground
The eagle flies, makes her round

Above the trees, shady green
Stormy weather, cloudy days
The eagle flies,
And stirs her nest
Like lilies upon the grave.

William Smith

This World Is No Friend of Mine

One day I will die
I'll take my immortal wings and fly
To my Heavenly home beyond the skies
This old world I'll leave behind
To live with Jesus – I'll be fine
Because this world is no friend of mine.

I want to see my Savior's face
After finishing this awesome race
When I enter the pearly gate
I hope not to be too late
There my reward awaits me
And surely, I want to be on time
Because, this world is no friend of mine.

Love Me, or Not

Why do you say you love me
And treat me like a rug?
Walk on me, stump on me,
Treat me like a dog
You can tell me that you love me
It's a game you play so well
The next fool that comes across your path
Is surely gonna catch hell.

You smear my name all over the place
Make fun of me
Right in front of my face
And to tell me that you love me
Is a total disgrace.

Why do you say you love me
Tell me those sad sorry lies
I see the hidden secrets
In those big brown eyes
You tell me that you love me
And that's a known fact
But I know for sure
It's the same old selfish act.

Customer Sitting At The Bar

The coffee in the pot
Just ain't hot
And de' bacon in de' pan is old
Waiting for de' bread, and the jelly
While the eggs, and potatoes getting cold
I've paid the bill
And it ain't no thrill
Lord bless this starving soul

The time is gone
And the day is long
And my appetite
Is slipping away
I think I'll arise
And tell that Bartender
I'll see him another day

Give me my money
And let me be
I'll go on my merry way
Come what may - I'm not gonna stay
Sitting at this bar all day

Girlfriend

I'm tired of being pushed around
And knocked down –
If I but had my way
I'd knock your head off
And dump you –
On the other side of town

But, because you born me a son
And my daughter is on de' way
I'll pray to my Heavenly Father
Lord! Help me through this day

You don't care how I feel
And it makes no difference to you
But if you were in my shoe's
Tell me, what would you do ___.

I may not be the best to be, you see
And I'm surely not your Queen
But what makes you so destructive
And so right down dirty mean

I'm not gonna find another man like you
And I'm not expecting too –
I have enough on my hands
Just to put up with someone like you
What do I do? What would you do?

The Echo Voice Below

Hear the voice of my soul – the echo voice below
Silent sounds of intangible words
Sought to turn your listening ears
Thus while you seek not to know
The voice of wisdom, knocking at your door.

Never, ever strive for less
Always try to seek to become the best
For where there is wisdom, there is hope
Tho' sometimes you just can't cope
Oh' hear the voice, my son
Because thou life has only begun.

Why Me?

My life seems like a joke
Sometimes I laugh,
And sometimes I choke

I pay my bills ahead of time
Check my account
Doing just fine

But every time I climb upon my feet
Something else comes –
And knocks me out of my seat –
Why Me?

The Only One But You

Your skin is so black
Your eyes so blue
Your lips so red
And your hair is too

I am glad I found
Someone like you
It doesn't seem true

I am the only one that loves you
The only one, but you

William Smith

Me, Myself and I

Me, Myself and I
Sat down to eat some pie
I thought I'd die
I started to cry –
There was only one piece of pie
For Me, Myself and I

William Smith

Good Looks

Good looks won't make you
But it will surely break you
You only pay for what you see.

And what you see
Is not what it will always be.

The smooth skin, the pretty face
Nothing seems, out of place
Catches up with time –
And soon becomes a disgrace.

Poor Man

I do not know
Where life will take me
But I do know for sure
It has already broken me.

I sleep in the streets
In the middle of the night
It appears to me;
It just ain't right!

No clothes to wear, no food to eat
No stockings to put on my cold feet
Poor man taxes
Is too hard to bare
I can't even afford, to cut my hair.

3 Blind Men

The first blind man says –
I can see you
In my heart

The second blind man says –
I can see you
In my thoughts

The third blind man says –
I wish I could see
The both of you...

Unfortunately, it just ain't true
I think it's a bad call –
Because I can't see . . .
Either of you at all.

Who Cares

The war in Iraq
Is truly a fact.
With bombs flying through the air
While soldiers dying everywhere
I wonder who really cares

The crying of infuriated lives in the streets
Dead cadaver disguised with prolix white sheets
There is no peace in the Middle East
And I wonder who really cares

Ancient buildings decaying each day
A price we will have to pay
We need to turn to God and pray
I wonder who really cares

We see the lives of many die
In this blood streaming war
Of children, and babies crying from afar
Everyone is carrying a gun
Someone's daughter, or someone's son
A nation, a people on the run
I wonder who really cares

A peaceful nation we hope to see
A stabilized country needs to be
Only pain, sorrow and misery
And I wonder who really cares

Tell Me What It's All About

I remembered when we first started out
A handclap – A song, then a shout
Tell me what it's all about

Together we both found the Lord
When de' bills were due, and times were hard
We had sung a song, a verse or two
Spoke in tongues, words untrue

A handclap – A song, then a shout
Tell me what it's all about

We rolled the floor
Danced the jig
Kicked off our shoes
And lost our wig
We jumped, we cried
We laughed, and we lied

A handclap   A song, then a shout
Tell me what it's all about

Church Goer

Church is not the place for me
What I see – is not suppose to be!
The Preacher running Silly Sally
And the Deacon smoking dope,
In de' dark old alley.

The usher on the floor
Slips out de- back door
And de' church Mother shooting dice
In the middle of de' floor!

Church is not the place for me –
What I see – I choose not to be
The musicians playing funk music,
Dat' is sick to my ears
This is what I had to put up with –
For 100 years
And what I've seen
Causes me to shed some tears.

I've got to leave this place
Before I fall on my face
Because what I see is a total disgrace
If de' Lord would call my name,
And beckon me to come,
Heaven could be my cottage
But hell would be my home.

Give Me A Break

I work all day
To bring home my pay
But you want me to wash –
De' car on a cold, cold day
How much more do you think I can take
Come on, give me a break!

I empty de' trash
And mop de' floor
Paint de' wall
And then some more
Oh' come on, come on, give me a break!

I wash de' dishes
And make up de' bed
Pay the bills, ain't nothing said
Come on, just give me a break!

I walk de' dog
And feed de' cat
I scrub your feet
And scratch your back
Come on, give me a break!

I brush your teeth
And comb your hair
And to me – It's just ain't fair
Oh' come on, come on, come on,
Give me a break!

William Smith

I didn't marry you –
To be your love slave
If I keep it up
I'll be buried in my grave
Oh' come on, please, please, please
Give me a break!

My Soul From Sin

T'was Jesus saved my soul from sin
And bought me to His mercy seat
To reconcile me unto Himself again
I was lost in this world undone
With opened arms, He welcomed me
With blind eyes, now I can see.

The glorious splendid beauty –
Of God's amazing grace
A glo' of righteousness forever shines,
Upon this mortal face.

Sin no longer has its reign
To Thee, I lift up my voice with praise –
Till life passes beyond its final stage
Escape the pain, sorrow, and misery
As I await for my immortal wings to fly
To my divine home in the sky
Into God's bosom, rest eternally.

Preacher, Preach the Word

Preach the Word to every human soul
Of God's divine grace, and mercy unfold
While you strive to win the ejective heart
May God's anointing never depart
So may your mouth speak of wisdom flow
Through broken hearts, may virtue glow

To share the Good News to every foe
Across the sky, and earth below
There, too, may you find peace and love
From God, the Father, who reigns above

Let your soul rejoice, your heart is glad
And every hungry soul be fed
Until the final day is done
Before the throne of Great reward
When we shall all gather on one accord
Let no temptation sway your faith
So – to deter you away from Heaven's gate

Arise, above the sinful tide
Anchor thyself, let God abide
Until you have landed on God's great shore
Preach the Word, and then some more.

Hey Man

Hey man
What's happening?
It's on the streets-
The drugs, the thugs
And the crack heads
Nobody's your friend

There's no good under the sun
Everyone seems to be carrying-
A loaded gun

Hey man-It's no fun
What's happening?
Little Jonnie Blue selling dope
And simple Sally Sue-
Hooking school-
It ain't no hope-hey man

The eagle flies today
And the card game players
Teaming up to get my pay
Praying that I can make it through the day

Hey man-
I've just gotten paid
And man, I'm broke
My car is being repossessed
And it ain't no joke
The credit card people-

William Smith

Is calling me on the phone
And the bill collectors-
Won't leave me alone

Hey man-
What's I'm gonna do?
I won't have a house to live in
A bed to sleep in
A car to ride in
I'm skating on banana peels-
And walking on my tipsy toes, and heels
Hey man-
It's nothing but dirty, low -down, sin!

Drug Addict

Brother Man-
I'm hanging on the edge of my rope
Drinking booze
And smoking dope

Don't leave me much hope
I need help and I need it fast
If I don't get it
I just won't last
Time is running out for me
I want to live-
I wanna be free

Brother Man- Hey Yo!
If I go down without no hope
Call de' doctor-
And call de' pope

Read me my "Hails Mary"
And let me ride
I'll hope to make it up
On the other side-
Just let me ride, ride, ride, I'm tired

Brother Man- Can't you see
It's no game- it's reality, reality, reality.

He Died

He died and left nothing behind
Only two pennies, a nickel, and a dime
His name engraved on a tombstone
Just looking fine, and left all alone

A champagne glass
And a bottle of wine
A smoking pipe, a pair of dice
His name engraved on his rocking chair
He left home and didn't really care

His name engraved on a tombstone
Looking fine, only two pennies, a nickel,
And a dime
He left to his children
In the sands of time- He died

William Smith

Let the Chips Fall Where They May

Let the chips fall
Where they may
Call it what you want to
But I call it a day
Let the chips fall where they may

Man, I come to work
And I am tired
My wife has left me
And my poor cat has died

I've lost my home
To the real estate man
I haven't lost my mind
And I ain't insane
Let the chips fall, Let the chips fall
Where they may- it's pay day

I've got some money
I'll pay da' bills
I'll call for my dinner
Meals on Wheels
Let the chips fall, where they may lay
It's payday!

Printed in the United States
By Bookmasters